The milk we drink comes from dairy cows

A Dairy Farm

Melissa Gish

A+

Smart Apple Media

COPYRIGHT

Published by Smart Apple Media

1980 Lookout Drive, North Mankato, MN 56003

Designed by Rita Marshall

Printed in the United States of America

Photographs by Tom Myers, Tom Stack & Associates (Brian Parker, Bob Pool), Unicorn Stock Photos (Eric R. Berndt, B.W. Hoffman, Esther Lawless)

Library of Congress Cataloging-in-Publication Data

Gish, Melissa. A dairy farm / by Melissa Gish.

p. cm. — (Field trips) Includes bibliographical references.

Summary: Introduces the characteristics of dairy cows and their calves and the dairy farming industry.

ISBN 1-58340-325-6

1. Dairy farming—Juvenile literature. 2. Dairy farms—Juvenile literature. 3. Cows—Juvenile literature. [1. Dairying. 2. Cows.] I. Title. II. Field trips (Smart Apple Media).

SF239.5.G57 2003   636.2'142—dc21   2002042786

First Edition 9 8 7 6 5 4 3 2 1

A Dairy Farm

H

On the Dairy Farm

ave you ever wondered where milk comes from before it gets to the grocery store? Most milk comes from cows.

Some cows can grow to 1,500 pounds (681 kg). The average cow gives five gallons (19 l) of milk every day. It takes a lot of work to care for **dairy** cows, and it takes a lot of space to keep them happy and healthy. All cows sleep in barns. Some cows are put outside in a pasture during the day. Other cows are kept year round in large, open barns. The cows can move

Cows eat the grass growing in their pasture

around in the barns, but they cannot go outside. Inside the

barns, cows eat from long, open containers called bunks.

Food for dairy cows is usually kept in tall, round buildings

called silos. Corn, soybeans, hay, and even **Cows must be milked twice a day, once in the morning and once in the evening.**

green cornstalks and leaves can be stored in

silos. An opening in the silo lets the food travel

into a feed mixer. The food is carefully

measured and blended together like a giant salad. In one year,

a cow can eat seven tons (6.3 t) of this food mixture.

Dairy cows spend most of their time eating

A large group of cows is called a herd

se bathrooms. The floor of a dairy barn has slots

ws' body waste, called manure, falls down into a

basement beneath the barn. From there, it is pumped into a

storage pit. The manure is then used as **fertilizer** in the

farmer's fields. This helps crops grow.

Caring for Cows

Some dairy farms are small, with only 50 or 60 cows.

Others are very large. They may have thousands of cows. One

farmer cannot care for so many cows. He or she needs the help

of farmhands. A farmhand keeps the cows clean, feeds them,

and helps the farmer milk them. ○○ Milk testers check the

milk to make sure it is good. They also measure the milk and

keep track of how much milk each cow gives. A single cow

This farm has several large barns for cows

can give enough milk in one day to fill about 90 glasses.

Some dairy farmers test their own milk, but large dairy farms

often need more than one person to test milk. Animal

doctors, called veterinarians or "vets," are **Jersey cows give milk rich in**

needed to keep dairy cows healthy. Small **butterfat, the creamy part of**

farms may need a doctor to visit the herd **milk best for making butter**

only once a month. With thousands of **and cheese.**

cows to care for, a large dairy farm may hire a doctor to work

at the farm every day.

Modern Dairies

Dairy farmers used to milk cows by hand, but now

most farmers use automatic milking machines. A pump gently

Milking a cow requires strong hands

pulls and squeezes the milk from the cow, just like a calf sucking. ༄ Dairy cows are milked in a special part of the dairy farm called a milking parlor. The parlor must be kept very clean. Before the cows are milked, farmers must **sanitize** the parlor. When it's time for a cow to be milked, she is led from the barn into the parlor. A gate is closed so she can't leave until she has been milked. ༄ The cow's **udder** is washed. Then the milking machine is attached

Milk is heated to 165 °F (92 °C) to kill any harmful bacteria. This process is called pasteurizing.

Cows' udders may be washed with sprinklers

to the cow. As the milk is collected, it is measured. Then the

milk runs through a steel pipe to another building, called a

milk house. The milk fills a large steel tank. Here the milk is

kept cold until it is picked up by the milk truck.

Off to the Creamery

The milk truck comes to the dairy farm every two days.

When the milk truck comes, the driver takes a sample of the

milk so it can be tested for bacteria. Then the milk is pumped

from the steel tank into the long milk truck. The truck keeps

the milk cold. When the truck is full, it takes the milk to

the **creamery**. First the workers at the creamery sanitize

the milk. Then some of the milk will be made into such

products as butter, cheese, yogurt, and ice cream. The rest will

Milk trucks have special refrigerated tanks

be packaged into cartons and jugs. Another truck will take the

cartons of milk and other dairy products to the grocery store.

Once the milk has been taken away, farmers must clean

the tank and prepare it for the next batch of **A dairy cow gives nearly 200,000 glasses of milk in her lifetime.**

milk. The cows are waiting to be fed and milked

again. There will soon be more milk to test and

measure, and more cleaning to do. Work at the

dairy farm is never done!

Milk must be delivered quickly, while it is fresh

Making Yogurt

Yogurt is made from milk soured by good bacteria. With a little "starter" yogurt, you can change milk into yogurt.

What You Need

A cake pan

A deep mixing bowl

A wire whisk

1/4 cup (59 ml) plain yogurt

1 quart (1 l) skim milk

4 small jars with lids

What You Do

1. Combine the yogurt and the skim milk in the bowl. Stir it well with the wire whisk.
2. Pour the mixture into the jars and put on the lids.
3. Set the jars in a pan and put enough warm water in the pan to come almost to the top of the jars.
4. Find a warm place to put the pan where it will not be disturbed for eight hours.

You will find when you open the jars that the milk has thickened. It is now yogurt. You can sweeten your yogurt with fruit or jam.

Calves drink milk straight from the udder

Index

Words to Know

bacteria (bak-TEER-ee-uh)—tiny organisms; some of them cause diseases

creamery (CREEM-ur-ee)—the place where dairy products are made

dairy (DAIR-ee)—relating to milk or milk products

fertilizer (FER-til-eye-zur)—material that enriches soil and provides food for plants

sanitize (SAN-it-eyez)—to destroy bacteria and make very clean

udder (UDD-ur)—a baglike organ that hangs from a cow's belly and produces milk

Read More

Murphy, Andy. *Out and About at the Dairy Farm*. Minneapolis, Minn.: Picture Window Books, 2002.

Pickering, Robin. *I Like Cheese*. New York: Scholastic Library Publishing, 2000.

Thomas, Ann. *Dairy Products*. Broomall, Penn.: Chelsea House Publishers, 2002.

Internet Sites

Agriculture for Kids
http://www.fsa.usda.gov/ca/
agforkids.htm

Moo Milk: A Dynamic Adventure into
the Dairy Industry
http://www.moomilk.com

Dairy Farmers of Ontario
http://www.milk.org

Why Milk?
http://www.whymilk.com